Wnat Clients Really Want

(And The S**t That Drives Them Crazy)

The Essential Insider's Guide for Advertising Agencies on How Account Management Can Create Great Client/Agency Relationships

Chantell Glenville

This publication is designed to provide accurate and authoritative information in regard to the subject matter covered. It is sold on the understanding that the Publisher is not engaged in rendering legal, accounting or other professional services. If legal advice or other expert assistance is required, the services of a competent professional should be sought.

Lifestyles
P R E S S

Published by Lifestyles Press
14 St John's Road, Tunbridge Wells, TN4 9NP,
United Kingdom

ISBN-13: 978-0-9935431-2-8

To all the great bosses I've ever worked with.
You made this book possible.

Contents

Part 3: Putting it All into Practice

"The biggest, singular issue between the agency/client and client/agency relationship is a lack of knowledge, awareness and insight into each other's worlds."

- Mez Ford, Consultant Director, Future Talent Partners and ex-Head of Account Management, Designate

"What Clients Really Want" gives you that knowledge, awareness and insight.

Why You Need this Book and Why Your Clients Want You to Read it

Even agencies producing great work for their clients get fired.

I have watched countless agencies producing good, if not great, work lose clients due to a breakdown in the relationship between themselves and the client... and there are strong reoccurring themes as to what causes this to happen.

This book gives an insider's account as to what those key themes are, and how they can break the client and agency relationship, as well as what to do to take those relationships from good to great.

The themes looked at are those which are most directly within the control of account management. The client/agency relationship is by no means the complete responsibility of the account management team but account management alone can break it.

Since most suits never work client-side, or spend years agency-side first, it can be hard to truly understand the different pressures at play in client organisations and why it is that sometimes such seemingly small things can cause such large difficulties.

Even after seven years in account management agency-side, working client-side taught me by far the most valuable lessons I have ever learnt on how to be a great account handler and build strong client relationships. I would recommend to anyone in account management, who wants to be great at their job, to work client-side at some point, even if it's just on a secondment for a couple of months.

> In case it's not possible for you to work client-side just now, or you simply don't want to, this book is designed to give you the best possible overview of what you can practically do in your day-to-day job to work as if you *have* been client-side and truly understand any client's business, role and pressure points.

An important point to note is that in this book I largely ignore the fact that clients want great creative work from their agencies. Of course they do. That's a given and they wouldn't have hired an advertising agency if they didn't.

If an ad agency can't deliver great creative work which solves the client's business needs, they'll probably get fired pretty soon anyway (well, they will if the client has any sense).

2

Here, instead, we look at everything else that can break client/agency relationships; all the s**t that drives clients crazy; and how, armed with this information, you can ensure no harm is done to those relationships and, instead, make them excellent.

This book is written for those just starting out in account management all the way through to account directors. If you have been in the industry for a number of years, you may find some of the advice obvious at times as experience will have taught you a number of these lessons already. However, there is a big difference between knowing that we should or shouldn't do something and knowing why it matters so much. And without a true understanding of the "why" it is unlikely we will adopt or avoid the behaviour to the extent that we should. For the first time, this book provides that "why" from a client's point of view[1].

If you want to retain clients and take your relationships with them from good to great then you need to read this book.

---

[1] This book is based on both my own experience client- and agency-side as well as that of others. The behaviours discussed and examples used, therefore, do not come from any one source and, where possible, the advice has been formed by looking at multiple instances of the behaviour and then extrapolating the commonalities. The content of this book is in no way meant as an attack on any advertising agencies. I have a huge amount of respect for the work agencies do and my sole intention is to share the expertise I have in the area of client/agency relationships, in order to make agencies' lives easier and, most importantly, clear the way for even greater creative work to be made.

Part 1

The Basics That Can Make or Break any Client/Agency Relationship

Chapter 1

The Importance of Attention to Detail

"Little details have special talents in creating big problems!"

— Mehmet Murat Ildan

"The Devil is in the details, but so is salvation."

— Hyman G. Rickover

Yeah, yeah, I know people constantly bang on about how important attention to detail is in advertising agencies. But do you genuinely know why it's so important? As in *really* know?

Are you sure? I didn't.

Of course, I had some idea as to why it mattered. But I thought the main reason it mattered so much was because, as an agency, you're the final stop before client's ads are supplied. If your attention to detail is poor in general how are they supposed to trust you to have checked their ads properly before supply?

But this isn't the main reason it matters. My incorrect belief as to the key reason attention to detail mattered did at least lead to the desired effect, in that I was always very fussy about attention to detail, but I only did it because I thought I should, not because I really understood the importance.

To some extent, I always thought it was a little silly because of course we'd check a client's final ads more thoroughly than we'd check a day-to-day email or the like.

It's only now, having been client-side, that I realise the main reason attention to detail really matters in client relationships is for a much greater reason and nailing attention to detail really can lead to more work being "bought" more quickly.

I cannot stress how important it is and how much better your relationships with your clients will be if you do this flawlessly *and* if you truly understand why it matters.

The main reason attention to detail matters so much is *time*.

Clients are busy. REALLY busy. You think you're busy in an agency? Of course you are, but in a very different way.

In an agency you're (probably) stressed, over-worked, on too many accounts and under a lot of time pressure.

Client-side, the extreme stress or pressure isn't the same. However, clients are constantly immensely busy with meeting after meeting as marketing teams have to manage so many different departments and stake-holders on any campaign, among a whole host of other responsibilities. This leads to most clients actually only having a couple of spare hours in any one day in which to review work.

As an ex-colleague of mine put it:

"Often agency account handlers are so focused on their area of expertise that they don't consider that creative communications is only one part of a typical client's responsibility. This is mostly down to ignorance and naivety but, unfortunately, this can also come across as arrogance to the client."

- Mez Ford, Consultant Director, Future Talent Partners and ex-Head of Account Management, Designate

Not appreciating the lack of time clients have at their disposal will always result in a detrimental effect on the relationship, since it shows a lack of understanding regarding the client's world and, as my ex-colleague pointed out above, it can make the agency seem arrogant.

The lack of time that clients have means that, if there is poor attention to detail in the work an agency produces, it results in a number of negative consequences for the client and creates bad feeling towards the agency for being the cause of that. It also has bad consequences for the agency's time.

The Negative Effects on the Client

You become a time leech

If your client has a 30 minute break between meetings and knows they've been sent a number of formats of ad to review, they're likely to set aside a portion of that time to review those ads. But if those ads are riddled with typos, mistakes and inconsistencies then the client will end up having to spend all of that time, if not more, checking and re-checking the ads again to ensure they've spotted all of the errors.

Why all the checking? Well, because it kind of makes it looks like no one has reviewed the work for errors before that point if there are multiple and varying mistakes in the different versions (this happens surprisingly frequently).

Of course your client would always double check all of the ads anyway, but they're only human so, to ensure they've definitely got everything (as the whole responsibility has now been put on them), instead of doing two or three checks they're probably now going to have to do something like four. If there are a lot of ads to review then that's *a lot* of time. Possibly even more than the 30 minutes they had free in the first place. The knock-on effect of this is that it will probably make the client late for their next meeting and they won't have achieved any other work in that time. Additionally, bear in mind that you are probably not the only agency sending through urgent work for them to review in those breaks if it's a big campaign.

This also means, of course, that in their next 30 minute break, they're going to get that whole suite of ads back through to check again.

In an incredibly large amount of instances, even on this second time round, a significant amount of the mistakes still haven't been corrected, or there are new errors, therefore leeching even more of the client's time and making them pretty p***ed off at the agency for not checking their work. It will also erode the client's confidence in the agency and mean that, over time, they start to review work with the assumption that it will be incorrect in some way.

All prior approvals are negated

There is just not as much autonomy client-side.

If something moves or changes in an ad, your client probably needs to get approval again from their very busy boss and even busier marketing director, if not another five heads of department too. Remember that all of these people are likely to have extremely full diaries.

This happens quite a lot as your day-to-day client has probably been told they're fine to go ahead with supply as long as the last change that was agreed has been made.

So, if something else then moves, the approval is effectively invalid and needs to be sought all over again.

I understand that designing means that if you move one thing other things sometimes need to move too (believe me I really do understand it, I've had this battle agency-side numerous times). But so frequently the things that move aren't because of a design reason. Instead they're due to lack of attention to detail and someone not having realised before sending the work to the client that an element has drifted into a different location.

11

So if you've agreed x will be in y location, don't just move it for the sake of it. By all means move it if you have good reason but not just because it accidentally happened.

Think of it as though the client's internal structure were like an agency; the marketing director being the equivalent of the creative director. Your day-to-day client's direct boss is the equivalent of the other most senior person on the account agency-side, i.e. managing partner.

If a designer had unexpectedly moved something fundamental on an ad you would probably need to seek the approval of the creative director and managing partner again.

Unfortunately for clients though, re-approval usually involves not only their marketing director and boss but also a number of other departments' managing partner equivalents re-approving the ads as well.

Again, this will make it appear to your clients as though no one has been checking the work properly and it will cause frustration on their part if they're being asked to seek further approvals due to sloppiness.

Other than creating bad feeling towards the agency on the part of the client, a lack of attention to detail will also cause further non-relationship-related negative effects for the agency. So it's in everyone's best interests to prioritise attention to detail.

The Negative Effects on the Agency

More rounds of amends, not just to correct the typos

When a client has been time-leeched and is checking multiple formats of ads for the fourth time, they're probably so frustrated by this point, and so focused on ensuring they spot all the errors, that they will not be paying proper attention to how each of the ads looks as a whole at that moment.

Until the errors have been corrected, agencies are not really getting the full attention of the client on the ads themselves. It's therefore much more likely, when this occurs, that late feedback relating to the actual design of the ads will come in. The agency then has more rounds of amends causing jobs to go over time and over budget.

Increased time pressure on the agency

If accidental changes have been made to an ad that weren't previously agreed to, but that the agency would now like to keep then, as mentioned above, this will more often than not result in the client having to go back through the review process internally for final approval.

Given how busy diaries are, and that this review process is likely to involve multiple departments, this may mean approval being delayed by a day or more. Worse still, it could also result in more amends due to people not liking the new change or spotting other elements they'd like to alter that they hadn't picked up on before (unfortunately the more times you show someone something, the more changes they're likely to make, even if they've seen it ten times before).

If an accidental change has made the ad infinitely better then, as an agency, you may decide a two-day delay is simply a necessary evil which you need to accept and work around. But, when deadlines are really tight, it is worth bearing in mind that the more things that change which hadn't been agreed before, the more time pressure the agency will then eventually suffer.

Given all of this, attention to detail is definitely not something that should be done just for the sake of it. It's one of the most important things an account handler can do to ensure the best chance of work being approved quickly and of maintaining a good relationship with clients.

Going Too Far with It

Having said all of this, it's also important to mention that there's no need to go too far with it.

For example, it's frequently suggested, and for the main part correctly, that meeting rooms should be perfect for clients. But this is sometimes done so obsessively, with chairs all being lined up the same height and the like, that agencies end up treating clients as if they're God; placing themselves in a subservient position.

Being subservient to someone isn't how you build a great relationship and partnership with them. And that is what the client/agency relationship should be, a true partnership, with everyone treating one another as equals and more importantly as people, since that's what we all are at the end of the day. The best client/agency relationships are always equal with everyone treating one another in a respectful manner.

So, whilst it is important to set meeting rooms up to the extent of making sure they're tidy, the reason to do it is not because clients should be treated as God-like figures; it's simply because people are likely to function more effectively in a tidy room.

The basics such as tea, coffee, biscuits and water are, therefore, also important, whether the client has gone to the agency's office or the agency to the client's. The person coming in for the meeting may have travelled a considerable distance or may have been in back-to-back meetings directly before the one they're now in.

We're all people and we do get hungry and thirsty at times, so do feed and water your attendees. It will ensure that they're in the best frame of mind possible for the meeting. No one concentrates well when they're hungry and thirsty.

It's not about pandering to anyone's needs, just about creating the conditions most likely to make a meeting go as well as possible.

8 Simple Tips to Improve Attention to Detail

I don't want to teach anyone to suck eggs so if you've already got the attention to detail thing down just skip onto the next chapter.

If you haven't yet mastered attention to detail, or if it's something that really doesn't come naturally to you, then this part is for you.

Attention to detail isn't a skill which comes naturally to everyone; it certainly didn't to me so I feel your pain but I can attest that it is 100% learnable.

So much so that if you asked anyone I used to work with, they'd probably say I excel at attention to detail, since I've spent years training myself to be better at it. And the more you practice, the easier and more natural it becomes.

(I say this fully aware that someone will now probably spot a typo in this book that has slipped through both my net and that of the proof-reader and will have a good laugh. But that's OK; we're all only human after all!)

Checklist for Improving Attention to Detail

1. If feedback has been given on a piece of work which is about to be sent back to the client for review, print the email/contact report out with the amends in *and* the last version of the ad that the client had seen and then check each element against the other. Never just rely on checking if all the requested changes have been made, especially not from memory, as something else may have accidentally changed that will, therefore, then be missed.

2. Read every piece of copy in the ad and look at every section of the ad at least twice, making sure you are concentrating the entire time. Even spell the words out in your head as you go, if it helps keep concentration, or look at logos and explain to yourself why they are in accordance with brand guidelines or not.

3. Review everything whilst actively thinking about punctuation and grammar. We tend so frequently to just assume punctuation and grammar have been included correctly but frequently it's forgotten in headlines and sub-copy, and even more frequently in T&Cs.

4. As boring as it is, make sure you actively look for the T&Cs on every ad to be supplied or sent to the client, even if there are 48 adapts. Then cross reference all of the copy to ensure nothing has changed. This is incredibly dull but, since a lack of T&Cs could result in a lawsuit for the client, it is one of the most important things you can do when checking an ad.

5. Be especially aware of instances where bullet pointed lists are used. Ensure there is consistency in whether they have full stops or not.

6. If there is a phone number, URL, call to action to search Google, a Facebook address or hashtag, *try it yourself.*
   N.B. With hashtags the check isn't so much to see if it works, like with phone numbers etc. but to check what it is currently being used for[2].

---

[2] Numerous brands have come into difficulties for not checking the tweets relating to a particular hashtag before using it. For example DiGiorno Pizza in the US tweeted:

"#WhyIStayed You had Pizza."

They didn't realise the hashtag was being used by domestic abuse survivors to share their stories, resulting in them appearing to be making light of the issue.

7. Print out anything you are reviewing. I feel bad for the trees in relation to this one but being able to go through a physical copy of something line-by-line and section-by-section makes it much easier to spot mistakes. Obviously, this isn't possible with TV or digital but I, personally, even do this with things such as contact reports, to make sure they're accurate and there are no typos/errors in punctuation and grammar.

8. Double-check anything you're even vaguely unsure of. If you're not certain whether something is grammatically correct, search online until you find a number of sources that agree (over time you'll also build up a great knowledge of grammar so you will need to do this less). If you're not sure if something should be spelled with a hyphen or an "s" or a "z", for example, the style guides of the broadsheet newspapers are a really helpful resource for this[3]. Style guides are like dictionaries but written for the reporters of each newspaper to clarify how different words should always be written for that paper.

---

[3] I particularly like The Guardian and Observer style guide for its ease of use, and lack of paywall, which can be found at http://www.theguardian.com/guardian-observer-style-guide-a

The Telegraph style guide is also easy to use and doesn't have a paywall but the guidance is more geared towards the tone and style of wording used in The Telegraph, rather than how each word should be written. Nevertheless, this can sometimes still be useful. The guide can be found here
http://www.telegraph.co.uk/topics/about-us/style-book/

I owe a debt of thanks to Matt Lloyd, Creative Director at VCCP Blue, for first telling me about style guides. They have proved invaluable to me and hopefully will to you, too.

Chapter 2

Over-Promising and Under-Delivering

"If people are honest about costings, timings and mistakes, you build a partnership that can get you through the tougher times of stakeholder management. Surprises and untruths result in pointless back-covering, wasting valuable time and resource and always a breakdown in relationships. From what I've seen and been involved in, this is the main reason why agencies get dropped or the seeds of moving are planted."

— Glen Price, Head of Marketing, HomeServe

Very frequently, work takes longer to develop than anticipated, be that by half an hour or even a couple of days. These things happen. Files take longer than expected to export or creative reviews don't go as well as hoped and re-works are needed.

Your clients, however, will make plans based on the timings they're given.

19

Sweat the Small Stuff

Even if the plans your client has made around when they expected to get the work seem very minor; i.e. all they did was plan to review it at a certain time and the delay is only very slight; it should be remembered that the smallest of setbacks can have a significantly negative impact on the client/agency relationship.

If there is a delay, the client will probably wait for the work to come through, which can mean they'll then miss other things as a result. This could be a meeting or something as small as lunch, if they have a canteen that closes at a certain time. I know, lunch! That happens really late in the day at agencies all the time.

You could say they should just suck it up and that may well be a reasonable attitude to take in certain circumstances, but bear in mind most clients probably have fewer options of when and where they can get their food, i.e. a lot are based on industrial estates so they do rely on canteens that have set opening hours. Stopping people being able to fulfil their basic human needs[4] generally speaking doesn't tend to make them too happy and usually makes them hold some form of resentment to the person who caused that state.

Also bear in mind that a large part of being great at account management is about making client's lives easier. Causing them to sit around for 30 minutes

---

[4] I refer to basic human needs here in the way in which they were defined by the psychologist Abraham Maslow who was one of the first psychologists to focus on how to make people happy. He argues that we have varying levels of need state and only once we satisfy the most basic ones can we move up to the next. Our most basic need states, as established by Maslow, are the physiological ones such as food, drink, sleep and sex. This theory is thought to be so integral to how we understand ourselves and others that it is even taught in business schools.

waiting for work to review and then being late for their next meeting as a result does not make their lives easier and can cause resentment.

Really Sweat the Big Stuff

More often than not, late delivery of work will have a much larger impact than just a few missed meetings or lunches. It will frequently mean that a client is left red-faced with nothing to show when they were supposed to review work with their boss or senior stakeholders, essentially making them look bad.

No one likes to look bad. Whether it is vocalised to anyone else in their organisation or not, they will be blaming the agency for the egg on their face at that moment; definitely not a situation which is going to lead to a happy and healthy client/agency relationship.

Err on the Side of Caution

If you ever have a choice between over-promising and under-delivering or vice versa, always choose the latter. That way, if you do succeed in pulling off a mini-miracle and delivering early you look like a hero.

If, instead, you don't veer on the side of caution and decide not to under-promise and over-deliver, you will always lose. In this scenario either you keep to your timings which is the expectation so it won't improve the relationship, or you end up late on delivery and the above negative effects occur.

As Head of Marketing (Project Red) at Virgin, Helen Tupper, put it:

> *"I expect them [agencies] to deliver on time and keep me updated as standard."*

Delivering on time will never make you look good; it just won't make you look bad.

It goes without saying to put a buffer into timings. Any project manager and account handler worth their salt will always do this as a matter of course, both for whole timing plans and just a single piece of work being sent for review. But it's not always that easy.

Sticking to Your Guns

What happens when clients really put the pressure on though?

You know what I mean; when they tell you it absolutely has to be through by 1pm tomorrow, even though you'd agreed end of the day, as otherwise there will be extremely dramatic consequences of some description.

It is so tempting in those instances, especially if given a tentative "yes I think we can make it" from the studio, to tell the client that you can do it but RESIST. It is so much better to stick to your guns and say that you will do everything feasibly possible to ensure they have the work by the new desired time, but be firm and clear that you cannot guarantee it.

Of course it's not as helpful as it could be to the client at that moment but, if they've moved the goal posts or briefed a job with extremely unrealistic timings, it's fair and acceptable to do.

This is especially true if you're being asked to put together whole project timing plans for briefs with unrealistic expectations on timings. By all means show the client how the timings could work to achieve their deadlines if everything goes perfectly and where there is buffer time, if any.

After all, giving a flat out "no" won't be helpful to anyone but be very firm and clear that if any one of those dates slip the supply will be affected and that could be due to the work not being approved quickly enough or even the brief taking longer than expected to crack.

These things need to be discussed openly, honestly and up front so that if timings *are* missed, you haven't f**ked up. Yes, there might still be some unavoidable blame as the client was hoping you'd fix it all for them... but nobody can accuse you of promising the moon and then not delivering.

If you decide to be the "yes man" and say you *can* make the timings it will, of course, have a temporarily beneficial effect on the client/agency relationship... but, if you then don't deliver what you've promised, you will have done much more harm than good. To have truly excellent relationships with your clients, you don't have to be a "yes man".

"Breakdown in communication between the client and the agency is one of the top reasons a partnership goes south. To elevate the relationship from vendor to partner requires more than just a yes man."

- Megan McDonnell, Senior VP, Pile and Co.

Have the Awkward Conversation

But what if you've already over-promised and are about to under-deliver?

Here it is essential to handle the client's expectations in advance.

Do not, under any circumstances, simply DISAPPEAR.

"...agencies, in a misguided attempt to keep the relationship rosy (and let's face it no one likes raising problems or causing conflict) either keep schtum or minimise the issue. But eventually, truth will out – and when it's late, off brief or hugely over budget, that small and potentially manageable problem is going to be HUGE in no time at all... Don't hide bad news – tell folk clearly and early."

- Richard Morris, Partner, Whistlejacket London

"When things invariably don't go to plan or there are unforeseen issues clients will, generally, appreciate a candid 'hold the hands up' honesty compared to an attempt to try and hide issues away as if they haven't happened or until a solution can be found. Honesty in adversity goes a long way and is respected."

- Mez Ford, Consultant Director, Future Talent Partners and ex-Head of Account Management, Designate

If work is going to be late, tell the client. The awkward conversation will be much easier than the angry one when they've been sitting there for an hour twiddling their thumbs or are just about to go into a meeting with senior stakeholders and have no work.

24

Always let clients know what's going on. Most of the time, the delay might not even matter, but avoiding their calls and not giving an update until you have the work *will*.

There is no way anyone can ever know all of the exact details of how late delivery might affect a client at any one moment in time. Therefore, an open and honest conversation is by far the best approach to avoid resentment and a breakdown of trust starting to build up.

Below is a real example of this disappearing act taking place due to work being delivered late. Have a read and consider how you'd feel if you were the client in this situation and how much a simple phone call would have helped.

Client Story:
The Great Disappearing Act

"I had one instance where, having worked an insane week, I was waiting on a Friday night for some work to arrive. I was told it would be with me at 7pm and I had plans that evening but pushed back the time I was supposed to meet friends so I could make sure I was still at my computer and able to view the files properly. I heard nothing until about 7.20pm and then was told they'd be another ten minutes or so. "OK, fine," I think, "not a problem". I know things aren't always ready as quickly as you think they'll be. A half hour delay isn't so bad.

Then I heard nothing.

It got to 8pm.

Nothing.

8.15pm.

Still nothing.

I call the agency.

No answer.

I email.

I text.

No answer.

I'm not arsey in the messages. All I say is I just really need some form of idea as to the new expected time I'll get the work through.

In the end, the work arrived at 9pm. The only communication I'd had, after that first "they'll just be another ten minutes" at 7.20pm was a phone call just before the work pinged into my inbox saying it had just been sent.

Bear in mind this was on a Friday night. *A FRIDAY NIGHT.*

I had plans, and I'm sure the agency did too, but at least they had visibility of how things were getting on to manage those plans.

I didn't."

Client, Anon.

26

I'm going to take a wild guess that this situation didn't do great things for the client/agency relationship.

Handling expectations and keeping the client informed of any delays or changes in advance really helps to preserve and build the relationship. It shows the client you are thinking about them and are respectful of their time and any other commitments they may have.

Chapter 3

Did They Get the Message?

"When you assume, you make an ass out of u and me."

— Oscar Wilde

If you had to cancel plans with a friend at the last minute and you emailed them to tell them but heard nothing back, you'd call and check they got the message or, at the very least, keep your phone on you, right? Or if a family member really needed you to transfer some money to them at a certain time, you'd call or text to check they got the money once you sent it, correct?

These basic norms of communication from everyday life also apply to client/agency relationships. Generally, if something is important, you check it's been received so, of course, it's assumed by clients that this is how communication will work between them and agencies as well.

Given this, the client is likely to get annoyed if these social norms aren't adhered to in the client/agency relationship.

And there are certain situations in which they frequently aren't. To make it easier to spot the scenarios that are most likely to cause a breakdown in communication, here are the top three situations in which I've seen this happen to clients.

The Risky Scenarios

Sending work then leaving

Work which is needed for a presentation first thing the next day is sent to the client late in an evening. The client is aware that the work is coming so they are waiting for it.

Having sent that work, do you then turn off your computer and leave the office, relieved your work day is over at last? Or do you give it five to ten minutes, then call the client to make sure they got the work and that they're happy with it?

All too frequently, the first option is taken here. The sad thing about this is that there is no point in everyone having worked late if the work supplied still isn't right for the meeting the next morning or hasn't even been received.

Staying that extra five to ten minutes to check the client has received the work and that it's correct, makes all the difference between coming out of that situation looking like a hero, for having stayed late to help the client, or a villain, since if the work isn't actually correct or hasn't been received by the client, then they're still left with nothing for their meeting.

Changing/cancelling a meeting

A meeting time is changed, or the whole meeting cancelled, even at short notice, but only an email is sent to notify the team. No follow up to check that the message has actually been received and that the change is OK.

The most astounding example I've ever heard of this was during a pitch process. One of the pitching agencies needed to change the time of the initial meeting so emailed the client to cancel the original appointment. That, however, was the only communication that took place.

There was no phone call or text message to check the potential client had got the email and, in this instance, they hadn't. So the client showed up at the original meeting time and, unsurprisingly, they were far from happy when they realised there was, in fact, no longer a meeting scheduled.

Assuming the client is working just because you are

Work is sent at 6/7pm that needs approval that evening, but it's sent with no prior warning that there will still be work to come through and no follow up with the client to check they've even seen the email.

The problem here is that your client might have stopped working for the day by this point and, therefore, will not be checking their emails unless they've been told that they need to do so.

The hours that clients and agencies work are frequently very different. It is quite usual in many client organisations for people to arrive early and leave bang on home-time, whereas at agencies it's the reverse.

It is only natural agency-side that the assumption is made that if you send work at 6.30pm your client will still be there to see it, since leaving at 6.30pm agency-side is positively early (I used to give myself a little celebratory high five whenever that happened). But, given the differences in the hours most clients work compared to agencies, this assumption is a mistake and can mean work won't be seen until the next day, unless it is explicitly mentioned.

If your client has left the office at 5.30pm and has no reason to expect more work to come through that evening then they may decide not to check their work emails that night; especially if they haven't had any calls or texts telling them to do so.

Never assume they will be there just because you are.

Many clients are client-side because they want or need a better work-life balance and will actively try to manage their time so that they are able to switch off from emails at certain times of the evening if nothing urgent is expected.

Just because they do that, it doesn't mean that they're lazy or work-shy; it may be that they have other commitments or need a more manageable work-life balance for personal reasons so *help them with it.*

Chapter 4

Liar, Liar Pants on Fire

"One lie ruins a thousand truths."

— Ghanaian Proverb

Lying in any relationship destroys trust and most clients, just like all of you ad land folk, are pretty smart, so it's reasonably likely they'll spot a lie.

You may be thinking "Well of course I'd never lie to a client", whilst imagining lying about big things such as costs but what about those other situations where white lies are frequently told?

One example of this might be a client asking for an amend that the studio and creative director think will look like s**t. Do you tell the client that their idea is a bad one or do you tell a little white lie and say something like "it's not possible" when, in fact, it is?

It's so tempting in situations like this (and there are countless variations on this type of scenario) to simply tell a white lie and make life a whole lot easier, rather than having to work out a way to tactfully let the client know that their idea sucks. But, as mentioned above, most clients *are* pretty smart and they'll know if it would or wouldn't be possible to move x to y within the current design or time constraints and they're very likely to know you lied.

A client that does spot your lie will, obviously, have a lowered opinion of you *and* your competence at your job, which will affect the client/agency relationship. Any trust that has been built up will be instantly eroded *and* you'll also probably have p***ed them off in the process (no one likes being lied to).

Precious time will also have been wasted in the back and forth of the conversation.

If the client has asked for an amend that you feel is a bad idea or if there's a similarly difficult situation arising, be honest! Tell the truth about why you don't want to follow their request… your expertise is what they're paying for so don't doubt your own skills and knowledge.

Nothing is worth getting caught in a lie for and the damage that it could cause to the relationship may be irreparable. If you work in account management you have to be tactful all day long; you'll figure out a way to tell the truth without hurting anyone's feelings.

Of course, part of the reason these lies get bandied about in the first place isn't just because it's easier to fib, it's also down to fear. You may be worried that if you don't come straight out and say "it's not possible" you will be *forced* to make the amend so that the client can "just see it" which obviously comes with the risk of the them selecting that potentially hideous version.

More often than not, though, if an amend does actually make something look hideous then a client won't choose it and you've built up trust by showing you knew it would be hideous in advance.

But what if they do choose the hideous one?

Then try to work out *why* and learn from it.

Unless you have an insane client (unfortunately, that does happen occasionally) there will be a reason behind their thinking and it may be one you haven't considered. It may be there is something which is important enough to their business/what they're trying to sell that it makes the reduction in aesthetic value worth it for them in that instance.

N.B. Remember trying to sell their product or service is the bottom line aim (I say this knowing there are varying reasons for advertising campaigns, such as brand building etc., but at the end of the day the aim of all marketing and advertising eventually comes back down to the same thing of trying to sell a product or service at the core).

As Ogilvy said:

"If it doesn't sell, it isn't creative."

Chapter 5

Money, Money, Money

"When a client is in a bind, do what you can to be flexible and helpful without mentioning payment or the number of billable hours. It's important that you don't get taken advantage of but making the conscious decision not to nickel and dime your client for that extra few hundred dollars you should have billed them for will come back to you tenfold."

— Mike Kapetanovic, Managing Director,
LMO Advertising

It is an inevitable part of our industry that things can, and quite often do, change. A legal restriction can sometimes rear its ugly head at the last minute and prices/products can change in the final stages of development. These things happen; even when everyone working on a brief has done all they can to ensure that they don't.

And, of course, hand in hand with those unforeseen changes come rounds of amends that weren't factored in to the original estimate.

If the additional change will take 30 minutes and is pretty quick and easy, I would strongly recommend taking heed of the quote at the start of this chapter and "*do what you can to be flexible*". Charging an extra £50 to a client, for half an hour of someone's time for a small amend, is really not likely to promote good feeling towards the agency. The loss of £50 worth of time is also minimal; it's worth the trade off.

If there are larger amends that need to be made, however, this will probably have a significant impact on time spent on the job and, therefore, costs will inevitably change and do need to be discussed as soon as you think they're going to be an issue. Ensure this conversation is prioritised and don't let time pressure sidetrack the question of budget changes.

It needs to be prioritised. ALWAYS.

Handling your clients' expectations where money is concerned is essential; even if you don't have time for a formal estimate with a cost breakdown, it's vital that you at least send an email with a ballpark figure of what the extra costs are likely to be... then there won't be any nasty surprises for your client and they will be able to effectively manage their budget.

This is so important; as it may be that if an amend is going to cost the client thousands, but they'd envisaged it to be minor, the monetary trade off will not be worth them proceeding with the amend.

I have heard so many gripes from clients over the years, thinking their agencies are expensive, and these gripes most frequently come from those times when clients are hit with large additional costs after work has been completed, with no mention of them in advance.

By doing this, the client is put in a difficult position, as they can't manage their budgets effectively with no prior visibility of costs, so will develop ill feeling towards the agency for being the ones to put them in that situation. The overall resounding impression will also be that the agency is really expensive and just trying to get as much money out of the client as possible, since additional costs that are not pre-agreed keep appearing.

Over time, that's going to make the client want to ask another agency, who is up-front with costs, to do more of their work than the agency who whacks down a shock bill at the end of each job.

Think no agency would actually do that on a regular basis?

Below is a real example of this mismanagement of costs in action.

Client Story: Paying For Their Mistakes

"I used to work with an agency who not only would send through additional costs constantly after the fact but who would actually, in these additional costs, charge for rounds of amends that were only needed because they hadn't implemented the agreed changes or because there were mistakes in the ads, such as typos.

I was so astounded that they'd try to charge us back for what were essentially their failings that I almost wanted to applaud the person who did it multiple times for having the balls to do so. As well as wanting to fire them on the spot for being so moronic."
Client, Anon.

Chapter 6

The Third Party Trap

Clients hire agencies because they want great creative ideas. But if that was all they wanted they could hire creatives themselves and have the marketing team act as account handlers.

The reason this doesn't happen (generally) is because agencies provide a lot more value to clients than just great creative work; which is also why accounts can be lost so easily even if the creative work is great.

One of these additional things agencies do, or should do, is alleviate the pressure on marketing teams.

A really good agency, and especially the account team, will always make a client's life easier. If it's not made easier, or worse if it's made harder, clients start questioning the value of the service they're receiving.

This is why the seemingly basic things considered in the chapters before this are so important in order to ensure the client/agency relationship doesn't break down. They're the things that, done badly, can make client's lives harder, but done well can make their lives so much easier and you, the agency and account handler, indispensable.

Given this, it's incredibly important that if you, the agency, are involved in the supply of work *in any way*, even if that work wasn't created by your agency, that the responsibility for checking it is undertaken by you also.

It is so easy to unintentionally make client's lives harder when there is work going through the agency that wasn't created by you but by a third party instead.

This is because it is frequently assumed that the work is the third party's responsibility and, therefore, that once it is received by the agency it can just be sent straight onto the client.

Doing this, however, makes the client's life harder if there are any mistakes in the work.

If you are in the middle as an agency, you need to add value by being in the middle or step out of the loop. If you're in the middle and don't add value by checking the work/amending any errors before it gets to the client, all you are doing is causing a delay in the work getting to the client.

The negative effects of lack of attention to detail will also come into play since, although the work is not yours, it came through you. Therefore you will be held responsible for any mistakes to some extent, even if just subconsciously.

If you are involved in any piece of work, only send it to the client for review when you think it is in a state where it has the best chance of being approved straight away… no matter who created it.

Doing this will ensure that instead of making the client's life harder, you are actually now making it easier. And, as you'll see in the second half of this book, a lot of the ways to take client/agency relationships from good to great are the things that make client's lives easier.

Part 2

How to Take Client/Agency Relationships from Good to Great

Chapter 7

Learn Your Client's Company Structure Like it's Your Own

"Get closer than ever to your customers. So close, in fact, that you tell them what they need well before they realise it themselves."

— Steve Jobs

To retain clients in the long term, especially through any difficult patches that may occur, it's not enough to simply have a good relationship with them... the relationship needs to be great. If the relationship is great then you and the client can weather any storm together.

One of the most important and beneficial things to do when it comes to taking a client/agency relationship from good to great is to really get under the skin of a client's company structure.

Client company structures are usually very different to those of ad agencies and, in order to be a true partner to any client, it's important to properly understand the dynamics of that structure.

By this I don't just mean the structure of the marketing department; I mean any area of the company that can affect and influence marketing, as well as how the campaign development process works for your client on any campaign.

The most basic level of this is probably already familiar, but really understanding it in detail will be a deciding factor in whether you have a good or a great client/agency relationship.

A spreadsheet which lists the roles, responsibilities and approver rights of all those involved in campaigns will not cut it for this. It will give you an overview but, to properly understand the client's company structure, you really need to sit down with them and go through what happens for them step-by-step on any campaign (or, even better, shadow them if you can).

Doing this will ensure you can factor in the points at which your client has to show work to x, y or z person, which of these people are allowed to feed back and also who gives feedback even though they shouldn't but gets listened to anyway!

Thoroughly understanding all the details of this process and the pressure points within it, will then mean that you're better able to provide the client with what they need at different points *and* better able to factor in the points when feedback will come through/how many rounds of amends are likely to be required as a result of that process.

I mention how many rounds of amends the process is likely to result in since if the company structure is such that all stakeholders are shown the work on first review, then you are likely to get consolidated feedback from the start.

This is, however, very rare since, usually, marketing teams will want work to be in a place where they're happy with it before sharing with the wider business and allowing other comments in. In this structure, additional feedback is likely to come late in the day so if you're aware of that you can factor it in.

This will take your relationship with your client from good to great since it will allow you to understand everything that is likely to be part of any campaign, and factor all of this in to timing plans, helping you to deliver on or before the deadline. It will ultimately mean that you can become a full and proper ally to your client in helping them navigate their internal pressure points.

Spending Time With your Clients and Why it's so Important

Getting to know your client's company structure like it's your own can only be done if you spend time with your clients.

I know it's hard when you're busy.

Most of you will have more than one account so getting the physical time to travel to your client's office, and the resulting lost time in your office, will sometimes feel like it's not worth it.
But it is, 100%.

Not only will it allow you to properly understand the client's internal structure, the pressure points they have to navigate and how to truly partner them on that journey; it will also allow you to have more face-to-face conversations.

The power of face-to-face conversations in relationships should never be underestimated.

If you spend time at the client's offices, creative work that would normally be emailed through and discussed on the phone can instead be reviewed directly with the client[5]. This means that you can hear their internal thought processes as they review the work and listen to their reasoning for any feedback; therefore putting you in the best position possible, if any of the feedback is prescriptive, to understand the thinking behind it.

Understanding the reasoning behind any prescriptive feedback is hugely beneficial for agencies, as it opens up possibilities as to how to address the underlying concerns of the feedback rather than just following the order. It's much better for you, the agency, that way as prescriptive pieces of feedback are generally the ones that turn into JFDIs[6] if the agency pushes back on them.

In order to get to great work and ensure that great work is delivered on time, spending time with your clients regularly is genuinely essential.

---

[5] I say this, aware that most initial presentations of strategy and creative work are done face-to-face anyway. However, usually, as a campaign goes further into development, these face-to-face reviews drop off and the creative is just emailed through.

[6] JFDI = Just f**king do it.

How to Find the Time to Spend with your Clients

First, ask for a laptop. A laptop, in this day and age and with the amount of hours people work in advertising, is not a luxury. It is essential.

Having a laptop that syncs to your desktop means you can get on a train anytime to go to see your clients and work on the way there.

Most people will have company phones they can even hotspot to remain online for the entire journey but, even if that isn't the case, a laptop that hosts all the same information as your desktop will mean that you can work on everything else on that journey (perhaps even getting the things done that your emails usually distract you from).

Secondly, you don't always need to go to the client.

You can ask them to work from your office one day a week or every other week. This is great for building a strong relationship with your clients, as being at the agency frequently and having the chance to sit down and work with you, will make them feel part of the team; with you, rather than against you.

As well as spending more time working with your clients, please, please also, for goodness sake, just TAKE THEM FOR A DRINK.

Seriously, you spend so much time talking to each other it's just not normal to not know one another as people.

Also, this will benefit you strongly in two ways.

The first is that you'll get to know your client as a person and, if you pay attention, this will tell you how they operate. What it is that makes them tick.

This insight into how your client's mind functions outside of work is invaluable. If you're smart enough to use it, it will tell you the ways of working that your particular client is likely to respond best to and the things which are most likely to make them love you or hate you.

The second way it will benefit you is pretty simple. It's much harder to be an a**hole to someone you like.

As I have mentioned many times already, we are all just people at the end of the day and we want other people to like us… especially if we like them. So someone is less likely to let their emotions and stress get the better of them and be a d**k to you if they actually like you.

Once you start to build these true, genuine client/agency relationships, the client's perception of you as an agency will also change from that of just another supplier to something much harder to replace.

As Jeremy Girard, Marketing Director for Envision Technology Advisors put it:

"If we do not engage with our clients in a real, personal way then we are just another vendor – and vendors are easily replaceable."

Chapter 8

Take the Blinkers off (ALWAYS Keep Clients Updated)

I used to work with a great head of account management who, before that, had spent years working as a client. He used to say:

"Always make sure you wake your clients up and put them to bed."

This could not be better advice for taking a client/agency relationship from good to great.

In Chapter 2 we explored why it's important to give updates if work is going to be late, i.e. handling expectations. It is equally important, though, to proactively update clients on a daily basis on any work going through and what can be expected when.

This is especially important in busy times.

Clients are kind of in the dark. They haven't had the conversations you've had with the studio manager, the project manager and creatives to allow them to get the full picture of what will be done and when.

If it's a really busy period with a big campaign going out, then the client will have a lot of pressure on them from all directions as to when work will be available to review, etc.

So help them.

Make sure your client always knows everything that's going on; what will be coming through each day that week, roughly when on those days, what will be urgent and what they can take a day or so to approve if needed.

This is so important as, if it's a big campaign, your clients will, no doubt, be spending at least half, if not three quarters, of each day in meetings. So help them manage the time they have outside of those meetings better. They can't manage it all on their own as they don't have all the information you do.

Something as simple as sending an email first thing and last thing each day with the status of all work going through that week, therefore, has a huge impact on improving the client/agency relationships as it makes the client's life infinitely easier. Doing this will position you as a helpful ally when the client really need ones.

I cannot recommend sending these regular updates enough but be careful that everything is included; not just the items that are most important to the agency at that point.

Sending regular, pro-active updates that cover *every-thing* going through at that moment will also help you, since you're then more likely to get the approvals you need in the time you need them.

How to Manage Urgent Approvals

If any urgent approvals will be required on a given day, when the morning status email is sent, tell your client that once you email them the work you'll call to check it's been received and leave a voicemail; but, if you can't get through, that you'll also send them a text message.

The reason for this is; if your client gets out of back-to-back meetings and their inbox has gone up to 100 unread emails, it will take a very long time before they happen to see that urgent email... by which time the deadline may have passed.

They may not get the voicemail straight away either since, if they know there will be some urgent emails within their now overflowing inbox, they're likely to decide to sort the emails first and listen to any voicemails afterwards so, again, they're still not going to get the message.

If you pre-agree on a text message to notify the client when the work has been sent through, they will know to look for a text message (which they'll probably get less of in general) and, if the title of the email is included, then they'll be able to go straight to the email in question. In this way, the text message will make your work go straight to the top of their to-do list.

Chapter 9

Understand your Client's Brand DNA Better than they do

Does your client's brand name have capitals at the start of each word if it's made up of multiple words? Is there a trademark symbol on the logo? What are the rules around how the logo can be used? Does your client use full stops on the end of headlines? What about sub-headlines? What are their brand colours and the variations on them that can be used? Do they have certain voiceovers for different products and services? What's their tone of voice? What's their brand essence?

To have a great relationship with your clients, it is essential to know the answers to all of these questions and more if you are the one who will be reviewing work from the agency before sending it to them.

One of the reasons this is so important is that consistently messing up things such as if each word of their brand name is capitalised or not will p**s a client off over time and make them think you don't know, understand or care about their brand. To properly nail attention to detail, a client's brand DNA needs to be so ingrained in your head that you even know it better than them and every time you review work you review it with that lens.

Messing this up will, over time, break down the client relationship as no one is going to trust an agency that appears not to know their brand, even if it is just in the simple things.

Not knowing a client's brand DNA backwards will also cause larger mistakes, such as presenting ideas that are against the brand values.

Doing this perfectly, on the other hand, will mean that all work and ideas presented will be in accordance with the brand values and, therefore, take the relationship from good to great.

Chapter 10

Idea Presentation and Development

"No matter what people tell you, words and ideas can change the world."

— Robin Williams

Regardless of whether creative work is good or bad, how it is presented is extremely important as to whether it will be well received. It also plays a crucial role in creating a good or a great client/agency relationship.

The way in which any idea is presented should show understanding of, and consideration for, all that is relevant and important to a client's business. Doing this shows the client that the agency truly understands their business and, therefore, can be a true partner to them in it.

Why a TV Script Just isn't Going to Cut it

It would be reasonable to assume that, with all the talk of integrated ideas that has been bandied about for years now, it would no longer be the case that sometimes creative presentations still start with one execution, such as a TV script or whatever the agency's speciality is.

If everyone really *is* buying into integration, then any creative presentation should, instead, start with presentation of the idea and then go on to the different ways it can be executed that are relevant to the brief/the best media to use to solve the client's particular challenge at that moment in time.

Even if not thinking in terms of integration, it would make sense for agencies to always start by presenting an idea rather than an execution because if a client just reviews a TV script, for example, and doesn't like it, then it's much harder to pull apart whether that is because the idea doesn't excite them or the execution isn't appealing.

If the idea is presented first, however, whether that is bought into or not is easier to clarify and then the execution of that idea can be assessed separately as well. This way, if a client doesn't like an execution then at least the agency knows the idea is thought to be good and to have answered the brief; meaning other executions can be developed from it, rather than having to start from scratch again.

The agency may well decide to start from scratch again anyway if the execution of an idea isn't liked but at least this process has provided more information as to what the client thinks would or wouldn't answer the brief and their business objectives.

55

Any great idea should have the capacity to be executed in numerous ways. I've actually worked on a pitch where the client awarded us, the agency, the work but wasn't quite yet convinced by the execution.

They did, however, love the idea. And it was a great idea, so we were able to go away and execute it at least five or six other ways (special shout out to the creatives that worked that one!)

Without an idea that was strong on its own merit and not intrinsically tied to an execution, though, we would not have won the business in the first place.

So frequently, TV scripts, or one execution in another type of media depending on the agency's speciality, are presented and the idea discussed within those parameters, rather than the idea alone.

Aside from hindering the creative development process, this also says loudly and clearly to the client that, as an agency, you're focused on yourselves and what's most important to the agency, as opposed to the wider spectrum of ideas that may be important to the client, e.g. retail windows, on-trade/off-trade displays, etc.

It's very rare that one agency is creating all of these elements but, because at least some elements like this usually exist for any client, it's important that any idea is strong enough to work across all materials that will be part of a campaign.

If there is one agency creating the idea, that will then filter down through all other materials being developed by them or others, then that agency needs to consider this and show awareness of it, even if it won't be their job to create that work.

When this is done well, it makes the client/agency relationship so much stronger, since the agency becomes a partner that truly understands the client's business. If it's done really well it can even, as I've witnessed before, result in the agency picking up more of the client's business without having to pitch for it.

This is so important that when asking a former client of mine what he values most from creative agencies, other than great creative work, he said;

> *"Understanding of the wider business objectives that the client team has to meet."*

\- Glen Price, Head of Marketing, HomeServe

Or as an ex-colleague of mine put it, when commenting on what agencies do that they have seen cause clients the most frustration;

> *"Not understanding the client's business thoroughly. We always bowl in with a certain amount of arrogance – giving advice on what we believe they should do, with only half the information."*

\- Anna Hristou, Founder/Partner, Wildwood Talent

Digital Banners Can Be More Important Than You Think

When the idea has been presented and specific executions in different media are then being reviewed, if your agency creates the online for that client, please also remember the digital banners.

57

Poor little digital banners.

They always seem to get left until the end, after shoots have taken place and there's no time left. As a result, the execution of them usually ends up, essentially, being a press ad split out into frames.

I've seen this happen both client- and agency-side on so many occasions and my God does it p**s clients off.

Yeah, digital banners may not be as sexy as a TV ad or as likely to win awards (although they can) but, as they're so trackable, they're usually a really important part of most clients' campaigns, especially in terms of reporting back results to the wider business.

Therefore, they really do need to be as effective as possible. Just splitting a press ad out frame-by-frame is boring and unlikely to create the most effective digital banners possible.

Digital banners need to be developed from the idea of the campaign and not from an execution that's already been developed. Only if they're developed from the idea itself will they ever stand a real chance of being properly tailored to that specific platform and, therefore, be as effective as possible.

Doing this will show clients that you truly understand the fact that any work you produce for them is about driving results and that digital banners aren't just a nice additional add-on. It will show you properly understand that all work you do for the client is of equal importance.

Part 3

Putting it All
into Practice

Chapter 11

Essential Behaviours to Start Today

The 9 Essential Behaviours to Prevent Damage to the Client/Agency Relationship

1. Attention to detail

Be as fussy as you possibly can about attention to detail. If you struggle with it then write a check list of what to look out for in each ad, from the "8 Simple Tips to Improve Attention to Detail" section in Chapter 1. Stick this list to your desk to make sure nothing slips through the net.

2. Handle expectations

If work is going to be late, by even by as little as 15 minutes, let the client know as early as possible and ensure a new estimated time to receive the work is given.

3. Allow more time
Always factor in additional time to timing plans, as things do frequently take longer than expected. It's better to be early on supply than late.

4. Stick to your guns
If unrealistic time pressures are being put on delivery, have an open and honest conversation with the client about it. Be clear on what you can guarantee and what you will try to achieve for them but can't guarantee.

5. Have the awkward conversation
Even if you know a conversation will be difficult, bite the bullet and have it. Whatever the situation, **never under any circumstances disappear**.

6. Follow up
Always double-check that the client has received any important message and pay particularly close attention when you are in one of "The Risky Scenarios" from Chapter 3, to ensure you don't fall into the common situations in which this breakdown in communication occurs.

7. Never lie
If feedback is given that the agency doesn't agree with, have an open and honest conversation with the client about it. Don't take the seemingly-easy way out and lie, even if it's a white lie.

8. Talk about money
Always give, at the very least, a ballpark of costs before any work is started.

9. Add value
Ensure you are always adding value in any interaction with the client so that their lives are being made easier rather than harder.

The 5 Essential Behaviours to Take Client/Agency Relationships from Good to Great

1. See your client
Ask if you can shadow your client for a week or sit down with them and properly go through everything that is involved for them in any campaign development. Then set a rule as to how often you'll see each of your clients and stick to it. For large accounts, which take up a high percentage of your time, it should be at least once a week.

2. Proactively update clients
Update clients on the status of all of their work that is going through the agency every day. Aim to make them feel as informed as you do about the development of any project.

3. Master your client's brand DNA
Read your client's brand guidelines again and ask them to give you a presentation on their brand values and essence. Then study this document and assess all work with this in mind.

4. Always ask "What's the idea?"

Stick a Post-it note on your computer that says "What's the idea?", then look at the Post-it note before any creative reviews and when preparing for creative presentations. Not only will this help with how you review work; keeping this question front-of-mind will also ensure you never present work where the idea isn't separated from the execution and clear.

5. Treat all work equally

Treat all elements of a client's campaign with equal importance. A TV ad is no more important than a digital banner or the like. All campaign elements need to receive the same care and attention as others. Any creative work should always make best use of whichever media that element will be used in.

Conclusion

Why We Do It

"Creativity is contagious. Pass it on."

— Albert Einstein

It is genuinely such a joy, both client and agency-side, when you work together as a partnership and team. There can be a lot of stress on both sides and being in it together to share the good times and commiserate together about the bad really does make it much better for everyone. And also;

"...if you enjoy working with each other you'll always create better work."

- Glen Price, Head of Marketing, HomeServe

I sincerely hope this book has given you the insight and tools needed to go and achieve those partnerships and great client/agency relationships.

As mentioned at the start of the book, I have largely ignored the fact that great creative work is required in order for client/agency relationships to flourish.

But do remember, you work in a creative industry. Have fun with it.

Question things, try to make them great, try to make them memorable, try to make them something that in ten years time you will still get excited telling others about.

Don't let the stress suck the joy out of the great things you help create.

It can be pretty stressful out there but, as one of the best bosses I've ever had told me years ago;

"Whatever happens, just remember, you're not a doctor. No one's going to die."

- Kathy Dover, Group Head of Brand, PR and Social, lastminute.com Group

If you would like to continue learning how to be the best account handler you can be visit;
www.MasteringAccountManagement.com

Here you will find a wealth of information on issues that effect account management, tips that will help you excel at your job and a forum so you can benefit from the collective wisdom of the site's community.

If you have enjoyed this book I would be extremely grateful if you would post a review of your thoughts on Amazon.

Most people don't bother to leave reviews but it would mean so much to me if you could take two minutes to do so. I personally read every one and would love to hear your thoughts.

About The Author

Chantell Glenville BA (Hons), winner of the WACL Future Leaders Award 2013, has worked at some of the world's top creative communication agencies, such as AMV BBDO, VCCP and Dare. Following this, she moved client-side, to Vodafone, where she managed numerous agencies at the same time.

Her experience both client- and agency-side has given her a unique insight into the situations and behaviours that can really break client/agency relationships or make them excellent.

Chantell has worked with agencies with varying specialities; from above the line to digital through to retail and experiential; both client- and agency-side. She has worked with a broad range of clients; from international blue chips such as Johnson & Johnson, Barclaycard, Molson Coors and Henkel through to high profile UK accounts such as Compare The Market, Metro, Gocompare.com and Vision Express to pan-European accounts such as Aer Lingus.

No matter the size or speciality of the agency, the same factors kept coming up time and time again, *both* client- and agency-side, which would cause difficulties in the client/agency relationship. This inspired Chantell to write this book so that others can benefit from her invaluable experience and insider knowledge.

Chantell has featured in the Evening Standard, in an article on more women being needed in charge and in Computer Arts Magazine, during her time at Dare. Due to her reputation Chantell has been frequently headhunted and specifically requested for accounts as a result of the great relationships she has built.

With the scholarship Chantell received from the WACL Future Leaders Award, she completed a Management Development Programme at the London School of Business and Finance in 2014.

Chantell currently runs JY Marketing Consultancy, which offers top level training for agencies wanting to improve their client/agency relationships and retain long term business. She also offers marketing consultancy services for small to medium sized businesses and gives seminars and talks for private companies and at public events.

For more information on the services she offers see JYMarketingConsultancy.com or contact Chantell directly on chantell@jymarketingconsultancy.com

Acknowledgements

This book is dedicated to the great bosses I have been fortunate enough to have in my career, many of whom I would class as good friends to this day; they have made such a large and positive impact on my life.

I also owe a debt of gratitude to all those who were kind enough to give up their precious free time in order to be interviewed by me.

I have been genuinely overwhelmed by how helpful and supportive even those who I don't know that well or haven't worked with for years have been. In particular, I'd like to thank Mez Ford, Glen Price, Helen Tupper, Megan McDonnell, Richard Morris, Jeremy Girard, Mike Kapetanovic, Anna Hristou and Kathy Dover, who are all extremely busy people but took the time to provide their extremely valuable thoughts on client/agency relationships so their advice could be shared with the readers of this book.

And to those who helped review varying drafts of the book. I dread to think what it would have been like without your pearls of wisdom and thoughtful advice. I'd like to give Rick Kumar and Dave Mannall a special mention here as they were both kind enough to read the whole book in advance for which I will be

73

eternally grateful. My parents have also gone above and beyond in their help reviewing versions of this book, as have a number of my friends; Phil Price, Sarah Ramsey, Olivia Roberts and Corinne Hitching. I will forever be in your debt for the support you've given me.

I also could not have hoped for a better editor in Lindsay Nightingale or proof-reader in Sophie Inglis. It has been an absolute pleasure working with you both and I very much look forward to doing it again in the future.

Printed in Great Britain
by Amazon

36558158R00050